Antifreeze, Leaf Costumes,

and Other Fabulous

Fish Adaptations

LAURA PERDEW

Illustrated by Katie Mazeika

Fish Poem

Fish live, hunt, hide, spawn-they've
adapted. So they thrive.

The archerfish sees its prey on a
branch: Ready, aim, fire!

And the blackspot tuskfish hears the crack of
clamshell against the rock. Did it break open?

An ocean sunfish enjoys tasty blobs of jellyfish and
the hammerhead senses its prey nearby,

While the minnows smell the alarm
from others-warning!

Oh, the fabulous adaptations of fish!

Fish have many fabulous and strange adaptations to help them survive. You might have heard that the ugly anglerfish of the deep, dark ocean has a dangling light in front of its mouth to lure prey.

And pufferfish puff up like balloons when in danger.

But do you know how icefish that live in the water around Antarctica keep from freezing solid?

1

Antifreeze!

It's not the same stuff used in cars.
Blackfin icefish have special proteins
in their bodies. These proteins keep
ice from forming in their blood.
No one wants ice in their blood.

Not even fish.
Brrrrr.

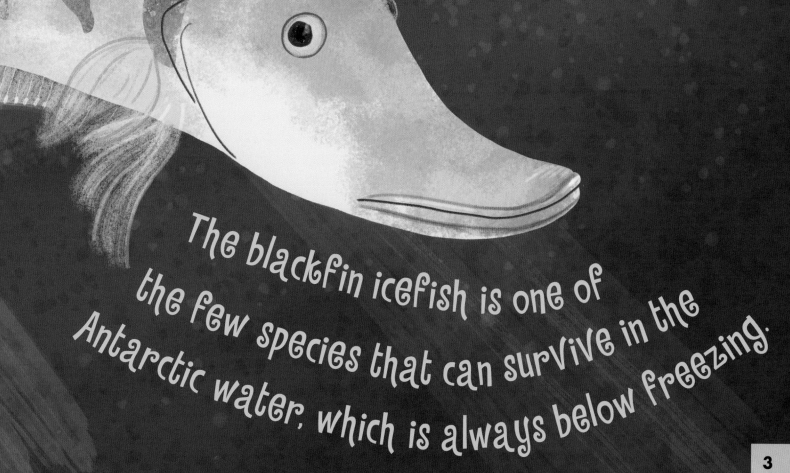

The blackfin icefish is one of the few species that can survive in the Antarctic water, which is always below freezing.

African lungfish have adapted
to a different challenge—
sometimes, there's no water.

Not a problem for these fish!

Before the water in their habitat
dries up, they burrow.

Then, they cocoon
themselves in snot-like mucus.
All cozy in their slimy cocoons,
they snooze until the water returns,
sometimes for months or

even years!

Lungfish have both gills and primitive lungs so they can breathe air.

A type of goby in Hawaii is another fish out of water. Nopoli rock-climbing gobies are, well, rock climbers.

Hey, fish don't have hands!

But they do have two suction cups—one on their bellies and one under their mouths.

They use these suckers to inch up the rock behind waterfalls to spawn.

These gobies are known to climb waterfalls as tall as 330 feet.

For a human, that would be like climbing Mount Everest three times!

The mudskipper can breathe air and can walk–but not skip!–on land.

Mudskippers also have to work hard to spawn. They dig U-shaped tunnels in the mud. At the ends are sealed, air-filled rooms for the eggs.

How do they keep air in the chamber?

Male mudskippers gulp fresh air from the open ends of the tunnels and breathe it out into the rooms. They have to go back and forth and back and forth **hundreds of times!**

Male leafy sea dragons have a lot of responsibility as parents, too. The dads have a special patch under their tails. That's where eggs are fertilized and left to grow.

After four to six weeks of daddy daycare, mini sea dragons pop out wearing their own leaf costumes!

How would you like to have all those extra leafy body parts?

Female leafy sea dragons lay 100 to 250 eggs at a time!

**Have you heard
about the fish
with four eyes?**

Okay, Anableps have only two eyes.
But they do have two irises and
two corneas in each eye.

This adaptation lets them see above and below
the surface of water at the same time.

That means they can look for food
and not become food at the same time!

This fish does not lay eggs!

It gives
birth to
live young.

Another fish with odd eyes is the hammerhead shark.

It might be awkward to have a head like that, right?

Then again, a funny-shaped head comes in
handy if you're a shark! Those wide-set eyes help
hammerheads scan the ocean for yummy stingrays.

Hammerheads also
use their heads
to pin rays to
the ocean floor.

Then . . . chomp!

Special sensors on their heads help the hammerheads detect the tiny movements of their prey.

15

Manta rays are stealthy predators, too. As they zoom through the ocean, they hunt by sight and smell.

They herd krill and plankton, just like a cowboy on a roundup!

Once the prey is corralled, manta rays speed through the mass of food with their mouths wide open!

It's a manta ray buffet!

Giant manta rays have wingspans of more than 25 feet!

Want to know how
archerfish get their prey?

Water archery!

That's right, they spray streams
of water like a super-soaker.

With skilled aim, they hit insects
perched on branches above the
water. The strong jet of water
knocks the poor, unsuspecting
insect off the branch.

Plop . . . Gulp!

The
archerfish
pushes its tongue
against a groove
in its mouth to create
the perfect jet of water.

Blackspot tuskfish use a different tool to get their meals.

How would you get a clamshell open if you were a fish?

Rocks!

These fish bash the shells against a rock over and over again until they break. Blackspot tuskfish then use their tusk-like front teeth (which is how they got their name!) to get the fleshy parts out of the shells.

Tasty?

Broken shells littered around a single rock show that the fish uses the same rock many times.

How about jellyfish for dinner?

That's what ocean sunfish eat. These
huge fish have teeth,
but they don't chew.
What do they do to get their
food into polite-size bites?

They suck jellyfish in
over their teeth.

Then push them out.

Then in.

Then out.

They do this until dinner is a
gloopy blob and easily swallowed.

The ocean sunfish can weigh as much as a small truck!

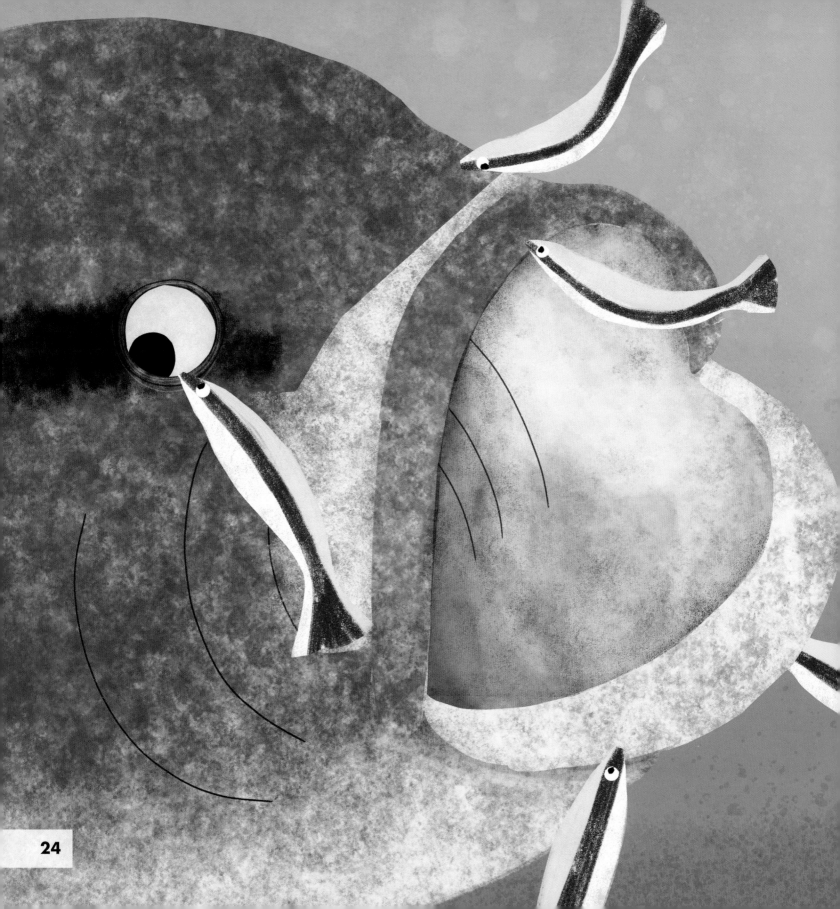

Who wants to know what bluestreak cleaner wrasse eat for dinner?

They love the parasites and dead skin
that come off bigger fish, such as the ocean sunfish . . . **ew, right?!**

Not for the wrasse. Or the sunfish.
The wrasse are doing an important job.

They set up cleaning stations for the larger fish and announce they are
open for business. The big fish get clean and the wrasse get a meal.

At cleaning stations, large fish open their mouths and gills for the wrasse to do their work. And they don't eat the smaller fish!

To avoid becoming someone's meal, fathead minnows always have to be on the lookout. These little guys don't get any bigger than three inches long.

So how do they stay safe?

They stay in schools—and you should, too!

They also warn each other of danger with a smell.

These fish release chemicals from their skin. This tells the others to swim for cover.

These chemical alarms can be smelled by other fish more than 12 feet away!

Fish have fabulous adaptations. And there are lots of other fish in the sea.

What fish adaptations can you discover?

Activity Time!

Write a Fabulous Fish Book

Fish have many different fabulous adaptations that help them survive in environments all around the earth. Write about them!

Anablep fish

WHAT YOU NEED

6 pieces of white paper, colored pencils or crayons, research materials (books or the internet), help from a grownup

WHAT YOU DO

It's your turn to write a fabulous fish adaptations picture book! Research five fish. For each one, find three adaptations. How does the fish hunt? How do they stay safe? How do they move? How do they spawn? How do they take care of their young?

Draw one fish per piece of paper. Be sure to put a title at the top of the page so your readers know what fish you researched. Then, write the adaptations that you learned about for each fish. When the pages are done, put them together. Use your last piece of paper as a cover. Add a title and illustrate it. Be sure to include your name as the author! When you are finished, share your picture book with family and friends.

If you use a binder or paperclip to keep your book together, you can add pages. What other fabulous fish adaptations can you find?

Leafy sea dragon

28

Glossary

Ocean sunfish

adaptation: something about a plant or animal that helps it survive in its habitat.

burrow: to dig.

chemical: a substance that has certain features that can react with other substances.

cocoon: a protective covering.

cornea: the outer layer of an eye.

environment: the area in which something lives.

fertilize: to join female and male cells to make babies.

gills: an animal part that lets the creature get oxygen out of the water to breathe.

habitat: an area that a plant or animal calls home.

iris: the part of the eye that has color in it.

krill: a small, shrimp-like creature.

mucus: a slippery substance produced in bodies.

nutrients: substances in food, water, and soil that living things need to live and grow.

parasite: a living thing that feeds off another living thing.

plankton: tiny, floating plants and animals.

predator: an animal that hunts another animal for food.

prey: an animal that is hunted and eaten by another animal.

proteins: nutrients that are essential to the growth and repair of cells in the body.

spawn: to produce eggs or young.

species: a group of living things that are closely related and produce young.

stealthy: sneaky.

Hammerhead shark

Giant moray eel getting a cleaning from a bluestreak cleaner wrasse

29

CHECK OUT THE OTHER TITLES IN THIS SET!

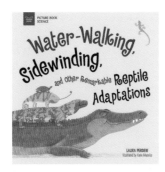

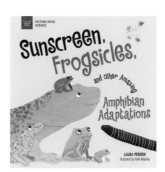

Nomad Press

A division of Nomad Communications

10 9 8 7 6 5 4 3 2 1

This book was manufactured by CGB Printers, North Mankato, Minnesota, United States
August 2020, Job #300938
ISBN Softcover: 978-1-61930-956-2
ISBN Hardcover: 978-1-61930-953-1

Educational Consultant, Marla Conn

Questions regarding the ordering of this book should be addressed to
Nomad Press
2456 Christian St., White River Junction, VT 05001
www.nomadpress.net

Printed in the United States.